WHY DOES MY
DOG
DO THAT?

This edition published in 2024
By SJG Publishing, HP22 6NF, UK.

All information in this publication is for educational and
informational purposes. It is not intended as a substitute
for professional advice. Should you decide to act upon any
information in this publication, you do so at your own risk.
While the information in this publication has been verified
to the best of our abilities, we cannot guarantee that there
are no mistakes or errors.

Author: Helen Vaux
Design: Blackbird Brands
Cover design: Milestone Creative
Photographs: Under licence from Shutterstock.com

ISBN: 978-1-913004-97-2

Printed in China

10 9 8 7 6 5 4 3 2 1

Contents

"Why does
watching
a dog be a dog
fill one with
happiness?"

Jonathan Safran Foer

Introduction

Bring a dog into your home and soon you won't be able to imagine a time without them. They become part of the family, and, like any family member, they have their own personality, likes, dislikes and quirks. Each dog's personality and character are unique to them.

If you've recently discovered the joys of a fur baby, you might find yourself asking 'Why does my dog do that?' You might experience wonder, confusion – or sometimes horror! – if you've had a dog for years and you think you know them well, they will still throw you the occasional curveball. You can't rest on your laurels!

The good news is that your dog's personality doesn't have to be a mystery. You can decipher even the strangest of behaviour. This book will guide you through all your questions, reassure you where necessary and generate lightbulb moments. The more you understand your dog's personality, the stronger your bond with them will be – and the happier you'll BOTH be.

This book follows the conventionally accepted theory that dogs form stable family units, or packs. There are other, competing, recent theories that do not accept this is the case; some studies show feral dogs form looser group associations, so dogs will swap, re-group or change group size regularly.

All about your dog

Stick in a photo or draw a picture of your dog!

Use the prompts below to record what makes your dog unique.

Name: OREO & BINO

Nicknames:

Date of birth: Dec 17th, 2020 & Nov 18th, 2012

Age when joined the household: 3 months & 1 month

Breed: Borador & Unknown

Parents:

Personality: Clingy | Independent

Likes: Food, toys | Socializing

Dislikes: Socializing | Being annoyed while asleep

Best trick: Lie down | Jump on your arm

Favourite food: Anything except Banana | Fish

Favourite toy: Spikey anything | None

Favourite game: Catch | None

Fears and phobias: ~~Vaccum~~ Monster

Funniest things they do: Getting scared of her own fart

Strange habits: Rubbing his face on rugs after meals

Doggy best friend: None

Favourite place for a walk: Behind John D. Bracco

Our doggy house rules: No jumping on bed, no barking at roommates

Nature

The debate over nature versus nurture applies as much to dogs as it does humans. Are we born with a particular personality or does our environment make us that way? How much does a dog's breed determine its personality?

Research suggests a dog's personality may be inherited from their genes. This is why we think of certain breeds as being prone to having certain types of personality. For example, Labrador Retrievers are known for being particularly bouncy and happy. However, genes are not solely responsible – environment and training form an important part of a dog's character. If a dog has been mistreated, they could be nervous as a result of this experience. While we like to think of dogs as relatively simple beings, they are in fact as complex as many humans.

What are they like?

Any list of dogs' personality traits could potentially be endless. After all, every dog is unique!

Timid	**Independent**
Confident	**Happy**
Chilled	**Cheeky**
Lazy	**Pushes Boundaries**
Affectionate	**Clingy**

Common dog personality types

The chilled one
This dog is very happy to enjoy life to the full. They don't demand a huge amount from you and are very easy to live with.

The alert one
Always ready to react, this dog will warn you with a bark if there's a knock at the door, a delivery van arrives outside or someone sneezes two streets away. They find it hard to chill out – there are just too many things to pay attention to!

The one in charge
Unlike their chilled-out counterpart, this dog finds it hard to fit in with human lives and training regimes. They're likely to be highly intelligent with a personality that dominates everyone and everything around them.

The nurturing one

This dog doesn't like conflict or chaos. They care for humans and other dogs and are eager to please, nurture and nourish.

The strong, silent one

This dog can be quite reserved and prefers to keep to themselves. They're the dog that the rest of the pack look to for guidance. They think they know best, which means they won't always do what you ask them to do. (We probably all know a human like that …)

Breed groups

The American Kennel Club classifies dog breeds into seven different groups. Each group tends to have common personality traits. You can learn a lot about your dog's personality by determining its group.

1. Herding dogs: have an instinctual ability to herd other animals (including humans!); intelligent; respond well to training; excellent companions.
Examples: Collie, German Shepherd, Corgi

2. Hounds: historically used for hunting; great at following scent trails; excellent stamina.
Examples: Beagle, Dachshund, Whippet

3. Sporting dogs: active and alert; well-rounded; need regular, invigorating exercise.
Examples: Cocker Spaniel, Golden Retriever, Weimaraner

4. Non-sporting dogs: hard to generalise but most make good watchdogs and house dogs.
Examples: Boston Terrier, Bulldog, Poodle

5. Terriers: energetic, feisty; high energy levels; can be very stubborn.
Examples: Jack Russell, Airedale, Bull Terrier

6. Toy dogs: big personalities; affectionate; sociable; full of energy; adaptable; protective.
Examples: Chihuahua, Yorkshire Terrier, Pomeranian

7. Working dogs: learn quickly; intelligent; strong; watchful; alert; great companions.
Examples: Boxer, Great Dane, Rottweiler

REMEMBER
Genetic inheritance only forms the basis of a dog's character. Your dog might be completely untypical of its breed. And, of course, crossbreeds won't fit into one box!

Ten happiest dog breeds

All dogs are a pleasure to be around, but here are the breeds that are well known for their positive personalities (and endless tail wagging).

Irish Setter

Bedlington
Terrier

Border Collie

Brussels Griffon

Beagle

Bichon Frise

Maltese

Labrador Retriever

Golden Retriever

"In order to really enjoy a dog, one doesn't merely try to train him to be semi-human. The point of it is to open oneself to the possibility of becoming partly a dog."

Edward Hoagland

Nurture

Nature and nurture both play a part in your dog's personality and behaviour. Whilst a breed might have certain traits from birth, the environment a dog lives in and the way it is treated will have an influence. What they learn from our behaviour – and what we teach them – is important.

The environment in which your dog is raised, the attention and enrichment you give them, their history, training and your own characteristics can all have an impact on your dog's personality. If nurture didn't have an impact on a dog's personality, there wouldn't be any need for dog behaviourists!

What can have an impact on your dog's personality?

- **Early experiences** (see The all-important early years, over)

- **Genetics** (see the previous chapter)

- **Health and diet**

- **Traumatic experiences**

- **Training**

- **Isolation** – being left alone and not being given the opportunity to socialise with humans and other dogs.

The all-important early years

Socialisation refers to the process of getting your dog used to different people, animals (especially other dogs), environments and situations they will encounter in everyday life.

Between roughly four and 12 weeks is the critical period of socialisation for puppies – they form opinions during this time that they hold on to for a lifetime. If your dog is no longer a puppy, any bad personality traits could well be down to poor socialisation. Of course, engrained bad habits can be trained out of a dog but it will require patience and time. Dogs are most easily shaped in those first few months of their life.

Finding a puppy

If you're looking for a puppy and visiting litters, it's a good idea to have a careful look at the puppies' personalities. (Don't be won over by sheer cuteness!) Always try and meet a puppy's parents. Are they friendly? Do they interact well? It's likely that the parent will pass their good traits down to their pups.

When you meet a puppy, how do they behave? Are they in good health? Do they look worried or appear overly shy? Do they growl or react aggressively? If yes, then don't choose this puppy. They are already showing negative personality traits. Pick the puppies up to see how they react. Look for pups that are curious, alert, playing and actively interacting with the rest of the litter.

NOTE

There are lots of factors to consider when buying a puppy. Never rush your decision and do your research! You can find lots of helpful information online.

Like owner, like dog

How much does your personality impact your dog's personality? Have they picked up quirks (good and bad) from you? Perhaps when you chose your dog, you gravitated towards one you felt was most like you. Do dogs and their owners not only look, but also behave, alike?

In 2020, researchers conducted a survey of the owners of 1,600 dogs (ranging from puppies to adult dogs), covering 50 breeds. The survey quizzed owners about themselves as well as their pets' personalities and behaviour. They discovered that a dog's personality changes over time and is influenced by their experiences and lifestyle. (So, if you have a Nervous Nelly now, they could be very different a few years down the line.) The study also found that owners' and dogs' personalities are often very similar. People with outgoing dogs, for example, tend to be outgoing themselves.

You are the centre of your dog's universe

You are the most important person in your dog's life. As the centre of their universe, your personality determines their experience of life. How you interact with the world shapes the way you train and socialise your pet, which in turn shapes their personality and behaviour. One study of owners and their dogs reached some very specific findings! It concluded that:

❧ Risk-takers were most likely to have Whippets

❧ Owners who are positive tended to own Golden Retrievers

❧ Extroverts often had Pomeranians

❧ Those who were very organised owned Miniature Schnauzers

❧ Affectionate, friendly people owned Staffordshire Bull Terriers or Jack Russell Terriers.

Have a think about the fellow dog owners you know – can you recognise any of the above? And dare you turn the mirror on yourself? In what ways is your dog like you?

You are the centre of your dog's universe

Parents are told to be good role models. The same applies to dog parents! If you've a tendency to be shy and avoid other people when you're out for a walk, your dog won't have the chance to grow accustomed to strangers (or their dogs). If you're always on the go and find it hard to sit still and relax — well, hello, fidgety dog.

Think about what behaviour you'd like your dog to learn from you. A calm, confident owner who is open to new experiences is more likely to have a puppy that develops the same personality. Of course, breed and doggy traits will always break through, but by being a good role model, you'll give your dog the best chance of being socialised and well behaved.

Remember, too, that your dog is quick to sense your mood. If you're agitated, they may react by becoming irritable or disobedient. If you're in a bad mood, wait until you feel calmer or happier before you interact with your dog. The best sides of your personality will bring out the best sides of theirs!

Ten dogs with the biggest personalities

A dog's silky locks, shaggy beard or perky ears are a great place to start, but there's more to consider than looks! Here are ten of the top breeds with the best personalities:

Labradoodle: affectionate, smart and great with children and other animals (including cats – although they might feel differently!).

Border Collie: with their endless energy, these dogs may be hard work and require lots of your attention, but they're up for anything. The fun never stops!

Bichon Frise: well known for their silly antics and having a fun-loving personality. Forever trying to be the centre of attention. Great with children and other pets.

Bull terrier: loving, loyal and the life and soul of the party. This dog always knows how to cheer you up.

Parson Russell Terrier: love hanging out with the family and happy to do anything and go anywhere.

French Bulldog: behind that grumpy face lies one of the most entertaining breeds. As happy to be active as they are chillaxing, Frenchies put a smile on everyone's faces.

Border Terrier: Sassy and energetic, they're the canine version of a 24/7 party animal.

Dachshund: these hot dogs are the whole personality package! Cute, cuddly, brave and very smart. And those little legs …

Pembroke Welsh Corgi: these fun-loving pooches are top dogs whether they're on the go, being silly or doing tricks. No wonder they were Queen Elizabeth II's firm favourites!

Boston Terrier: as well as being one of the most intelligent breeds and extremely obedient, they want nothing more than to have fun. Show them an agility course and they're in seventh heaven!

"Dogs do speak,
but only to those
who know how
to listen."

Orhan Pamuk

All in the eyes

Dogs have wonderfully expressive eyes – hence those irresistible 'puppy dog eyes'. Their eyes tell you a lot about how they're feeling. This can help you interpret what your dog is trying to 'say' to you (and to their fellow dogs) and how to best meet their needs.

Blinks and winks

If your dog blinks at you, it's a positive sign. It shows they feel relaxed and calm. Your dog will use the same technique to tell another dog that they're friendly and don't pose a threat. Try blinking back slowly at your dog – when they see you're relaxed, they'll feel even more chilled out. This can also help if your dog has a nervous disposition as it demonstrates you don't pose a threat. The blinking is key – staring can send difference messages (see page 26).

Are you curious why your dog lies with their eyes half open? It's not because they're prepped like a ninja to respond to danger. Quite the opposite. It shows that they're content and don't feel any need to keep their eyes wide open. In a nutshell, they trust you.

If your dog does rest with their eyes fully open, it doesn't necessarily mean they feel uncomfortable with you. It could be that something has changed in the environment that's making them feel a little tense. What seems inconsequential to us, for example a new piece of furniture, can leave your dog feeling unsettled. They're certainly creatures of routine. Dogs also have a third eyelid that is often visible as they sleep, so it can look like their eyes are open when they aren't!

Squinting

Does your dog squint at you? Are you wondering if they need a trip to the dog opticians? Or could they be giving you the side-eye? Rest assured, your dog isn't being sassy. Squinting is usually a sign of contentment, joy and happiness. When they squint whilst averting their eyes it means there's not a hint of aggression in them. The best time to spot squinting is when you're giving your dog a belly rub!

Staring contests

It's not unusual for a dog to stare and it doesn't mean they are being vacant. If your dog is staring, it can mean several things:

1. They love you!
2. They're reading your body language.
3. They're feeling confused.
4. They want something (including attention!).

Staring can indicate that your dog is unsure about whatever it is they're looking at. It could be a new toy, a different type of food or an unfamiliar person. They're assessing it and processing lots of information, just like we do when we see an object or person we don't recognise. It's perfectly okay and normal for your dog to be cautious of new things. Use it as your cue to make them feel more comfortable.

Who's the boss?

When your dog is excited about something, you'll notice that their pupils dilate and they fix you with a stare. (Think of when they're waiting for you to throw a ball.) However, this stare is also a signal of dominance. As soon as you throw that ball, you've given them the signal that they're the boss. Just think of that when you complain your dog never tires of playing fetch – they've got you wrapped around their little paws. And you thought you were the one in charge?!

A WORD OF CAUTION

It's fine to gaze adoringly into your dog's eyes – they know they can trust you. However, don't try it with dogs you don't know. They may think you are trying to be dominant and interpret it as a sign of aggression. Instead, when meeting a strange dog, minimise eye contact and talk softly to them.

Food, glorious food

What's your dog's favourite thing after you? Food. In fact, you'd be forgiven for thinking they have a one-track mind when it comes to food. Dogs can also have a very loose definition of what 'food' is!

Coprophagia

In other words, eating poo. This isn't uncommon in the animal world but that doesn't make it pleasant. So, why do they do it (and then proceed to lick your face)?

🐾 Some dogs will resort to eating poo if they're hungry.

🐾 Perhaps they didn't eat as much of their usual meal, they've upped their exercise level or they're on medication that increases their appetite. Dogs aren't as grossed out by this as humans are!

🐾 It could be habit – they try eating poo as a pup and it becomes normal behaviour. It can also be common for a female dog to eat her puppies' poo so don't worry if you notice that.

🐾 Dogs will sometimes eat poo if they are bored, stressed or anxious. (Thank goodness humans don't follow suit!)

🐾 Fancy a bit of attention from your owner? Eat some poo! If your dog learns that their coprophagic craving gets your attention, they can't help themselves. After all, being told off is better than no attention at all.

If your dog is eating poo more than usual (or they start doing it having been poo-averse before), it's worth a trip to the vets to check there aren't any underlying medical causes.

There goes another shoe ...

Most dogs will have a nibble at something they shouldn't every once in a while. But what if your dog is actually ingesting it? Eating foreign bodies – in particular, indigestible items – can be a real problem. It's even got a name, pica, which is defined as: 'the persistent chewing and consumption of non-nutritional substances that provide no physical benefit'. Humans do it too (Google it!).

Dogs have been known to consume various items, for example, socks, stones, candles and Lego bricks. But why do they do this to themselves? The reasons are similar to the stomach-churning poop-eating described above:

- Anxious dogs often channel their stress into abnormal eating habits. For example, if your dog gets upset when they're left alone in the house, you may come home to a deconstructed sofa or cushion.

- Teething puppies are prone to chewing on items such as table legs and even the corners of internal walls as a way of massaging their sore gums when their teeth break through. Human babies and toddlers are also guilty of the same (although they tend not to chew through furniture).

- If your dog isn't getting enough exercise, mental stimulation or social interaction, they will create their own fun to ease the boredom. What to you is just a pillow or a cushion off the sofa, your dog sees as a companion for a game of rough and tumble ...

As with coprophagia, it's important to eliminate any medical or nutritional reasons for your dog's abnormal eating habits. If you suspect they've swallowed something whole (where did those keys go?), it's important to get them to the vet as soon as possible. In the event they require surgery, your dog will usually be fine and recover within a few days.

What else can you do? Ensure your dog isn't bored or anxious. Give them lots of exercise and plenty of toys for mental stimulation. Toys are also a great way to help your dog redirect their desire to chew. The key is to divert those behaviours before they become hard-to-break habits and keep the inappropriate items they find so delicious well out of reach!

Fear of food ... or something else?

Is your dog cowering and shaking at mealtimes when they should be wolfing down their food? It's unlikely to be the food that is causing the issue, but it could well be the bowl you're using. If your dog has a nervous personality, certain bowls can really put them on edge, particularly metal ones. The sound of their collar or tag hitting the metal can be quite terrifying, as can seeing their own reflection. Try different types of bowls to find out what your dog is comfortable with.

A moveable feast

It's not unusual for dogs to transfer the food in their bowl to the floor before eating it. Is your dog being extremely picky? Possibly, but another reason is more likely: they don't like their bowl. Again, it could be the sound it makes, or the smell of the washing-up liquid you use. Another problem is a bowl that moves as your dog tries to eat – by putting the food on the floor, your dog can ensure it doesn't go anywhere!

Some dogs aren't bothered at all by a bowl that moves. Dogs with a high-energy personality are often so keen to get every last morsel, their vigorous licking will move the bowl here, there and everywhere. This doesn't mean your dog is greedy, just that they're full of enthusiasm!

If your dog takes their food elsewhere in your home – perhaps to their bed or the corner of another room – they're not being 'odd' or secretive. They're simply taking it to where they feel safe. This could be to prevent another dog, or even a cat, from laying claim to it. Even if that threat isn't real, they will instinctively protect what's theirs.

Slow eating

If your dog takes a long time to eat a meal, it's not just good for their digestion, it also means they're feeling relaxed. A dog that feels comfortable with their environment doesn't worry that someone is going to steal their food when they're not looking. They feel confident that they can walk away, and it will still be there when they return to it.

Note: if your dog starts doing this and it's out of character, get them checked out – if could be a sign of tooth problems or stomach ache.

Sucking

Does your dog suck on their chews rather than, well, chew them? They might do the same with blankets and their favourite toy. Canine behaviourists believe this personality trait is linked to not having had the chance for comfort suckling when they were a puppy. Perhaps their mother was unwell and unable to feed her litter, or the puppy was separated from their mother too early.

Suckling is an activity that makes puppies feel safe, secure and comforted. So, when your dog is sucking on a chew and looking like a baby, they're self-soothing – which makes them feel warm and fuzzy inside.

Begging

Why is your dog suddenly at your feet every time you open the fridge or sit down to eat? Dogs are opportunistic by nature. If they detect food, they can't resist begging. It doesn't mean your dog is a greedy rascal; they do it because canines are scavengers … and they love food! A begging dog is very hard to resist but resist you must! As soon as you give in, you send the signal that begging gets attention and food. And so, the cycle continues …

"I think dogs are the most amazing creatures. They give unconditional love. For me they are the role model for being alive."

Gilda Radner

Out for a walk

Off the lead and with the space to run free, your dog's personality is truly unleashed. You'll be treated to new levels of silliness along with their need for speed (however short their legs). You'll also find out how well you've trained your dog. There's nothing quite as embarrassing as trying to recall a disobedient hound!

Putting the doggy brakes on

Picture the scene: You're enjoying a lovely walk, there's been lots of tail-wagging and then all of a sudden your dog refuses to move. They're not going anywhere. Why this sudden stubbornness? You don't see this side to their personality in the house, so what's going on?

For starters, they could just be doggone tired. We've all been so tired that we want to collapse in a heap and not go on any further. Actually doing that would look rather odd so humans tend to soldier on until they find an appropriate place to rest. Dogs don't pay heed to any such social niceties – sitting on a pavement NOW is far more appealing than waiting until they get home.

If your dog has a nervous personality, they might stop to avoid something scary. Perhaps they've spotted a strange dog ahead or they might have an irrational fear of bicycles. Once that 'threat' has passed, your dog will probably be happy to get going again. Be mindful of what's going on around you and help your dog to feel secure until the moment passes.

Dogs also have a great associative memory. They remember people, places and experiences based on associations. This is why they get excited when you put your shoes on – they associate shoes with going out for a walk. The spot where they stop could have a positive association for your dog. Did they find a biscuit or spot a squirrel there once? Chances are they've stopped in the hope the experience will be repeated!

Puppies have a strong instinct to stay close to home. It's a genetic mechanism that ensures they don't get separated from their litter. If your dog is a pup, far from being stubborn, refusing to move is simply that natural mechanism kicking in. It will disappear the older and more confident they get.

Pee breaks

If you're forever stopping for your dog to pee, you'll have two questions: 'Why?' and 'How does their bladder keep refilling?' As frustrating as all these stops are, your dog isn't trying to slow you down, nor are they a nervous wreck. When your dog pees on a walk, they're leaving scent marks for other dogs to inspect – they're sending a wee-mail. Every dog has a unique scent signature so it's akin to leaving a business card. It communicates stacks of information to other dogs, such as age, sex, emotional state and even whether they're feeling a little amorous. It also marks their territory – handy for finding the way home, Hansel-and-Gretel-style.

Note: if frequent pee stops are a new thing, it could be a sign of an infection so do take your pooch to the vet for a check.

Why is your dog obsessed with rolling in dirt?

Most dogs will pick up a bit of dirt on a walk and not be bothered by it. They do, however, have a strong tendency to make a beeline for anything particularly smelly, messy and dirty if the opportunity arises. If your dog regularly needs bathing to remove something unpleasant from their coat, it's not a sign they have zero personal hygiene standards. They're just doing normal dog stuff!

But what's the big attraction about rolling in fox poo and other unmentionable substances? This behaviour harks back to before dogs were domesticated. It's thought that by rolling in strong odours, dogs could disguise their own scent and make it harder for predators and prey to detect them. Obviously, for our pets, this rationale no longer exists yet the urge to do it continues – and they get great pleasure from it!

TEN MOST STUBBORN DOG BREEDS

These breeds are unlikely to do anything they don't want to! Headstrong and independent, you may find them difficult (although not impossible) to train.

Afghan Hound

American Foxhound

Basset Hound

Bulldog

Bull Mastiff

Chinese Shar-Pei

Bull Terrier

Pekingese

Chow Chow

Siberian Husky

Why does your dog chase everything in sight?

Taking your dog for a walk can be stressful if they like chasing anything that moves. This can particularly be the case if they're off the lead and their recall is on the unreliable side. Are they trying to make friends? Or is something more sinister afoot? Is there an aggressive side to them that you really don't want to know about?

Many dogs – but certainly not all – have a strong chase response. This comes from way back when it was their natural instinct to hunt for food. In some, it's so strong that there's very little you can do to stop a chase and your commands will be ineffective. Fortunately, unless your dog is super-fast, it is unusual for them to catch anything. (Of course, they always believe they will.)

However calm and friendly your dog's personality is, this natural urge will inevitably overwhelm them at times. The best you can do is work on their recall, rewarding them when they do break off a chase to come back to you. You can also try to stay one step ahead of your dog, notice potential prey before they do, and slip their lead on!

Why do they jump up at other walkers?

When your dog jumps up at someone, they will inevitably do so with muddy paws. (That's just dog law.) Best-case scenario, it's another dog walker who will understand. Worst-case scenario, it's someone wearing brand new white jeans who's never owned a dog. Either way, it's a little awkward.

Dogs can jump up if they're trying to alert you to something, but if your dog's personality is attention-seeking and over-excitable, how can you reduce the risk of this happening? For starters, never encourage your dog to jump up at you as this reinforces the behaviour. If they do jump up, ignore them until they get down. Don't make eye contact. Only reward them when all four paws are fully grounded and all attempts to jump have stopped. This teaches your dog that jumping up isn't a positive thing to do – all being well, this will translate to when they meet other people.

Meeting other dogs

The interaction between dogs is fascinating to watch. Whilst they can be like humans in many ways, the way they meet and greet other canines is anything but. (Or butt …)

What's the fascination with sniffing bottoms?

When dogs meet each other, they love to sniff each other's rear ends. You'd be mistaken for thinking your dog has the social propriety of a toddler. Although it's entirely normal – and doesn't reflect poorly on your dog's personality – we nonetheless feel a little embarrassed. By sniffing butts, dogs learn lots of information about each another. So, let them get on with it and stop blushing.

If your dog (or their new friend) is getting annoyed by this behaviour, you need to distract your dog to put a stop to it. The same applies when your dog sniffs the groin or bottom of a human. Embarrassing, YES, but normal. Just point them in the direction of another activity.

Is your dog a complete wimp?

There are times when you may wonder if your dog is a coward. Things that don't bother us can be perturbing to a dog. Does your dog always roll onto their back when they meet other dogs? There are two possible reasons for this. The commonly held view is that they're showing submission, acknowledging the dominance of the other dog by exposing their vulnerable underbelly.

The second explanation is exactly the opposite. By rolling on their back, they're in a good defensive position from which to dodge the other dog and launch their own 'attack'. What does this say about your dog's personality? Well, they're either a wimp or they're cunning! Some breeds are more likely to be one or the other, so consider what else you know about your dog's personality before deciding!

Are they getting a little too 'friendly'?

Humping is a common doggy behaviour that can be excruciatingly embarrassing, particularly if they try to 'mount' a human leg. Dogs aren't fussy – furniture, toys and shoes are all fair game. They may become over familiar with another dog (male, female, it really doesn't matter) when you're out for a walk. It's not a sign that your dog is a canine Casanova. What's the rationale for this romping?

🐾 Yes, it can be sexual and hormone-related.

🐾 Stress – if your dog is stressed or overstimulated, humping is way for them to self-soothe.

🐾 Excitement or play – for some dogs it's just their way of burning off excess energy and getting attention (other, less embarrassing, dogs choose to simply run around).

Again, distracting your dog is the best way to put a stop to this behaviour, especially as there's no easy way to ignore it!

Let sleeping dogs lie

Dogs can fall asleep anytime, anyplace, anywhere. Then, at the drop of a hat, they wake up full of energy and raring to go. Let's look at what sleep tells you about your furry friend ...

Sweet dreams

Just like humans, dogs enter a sleep phase called REM (rapid eye movement), where dreaming occurs. If you notice your dog making running motions with their legs, twitching or barking softly, it's most likely they're having a dream. What are they dreaming about? Dog experts believe that doggy dreams are all about their everyday activities, so things like playing and chasing balls and frisbees. Dreaming helps dogs consolidate memories and process their experiences, just like it does for humans.

The fact that dogs dream is a fascinating insight into their psyche. But what does it tell you about their personality? It's hard to tell without seeing into their dreams! Humans tend to have vivid (and weird) dreams when they're anxious, but we don't know if this translates into the canine world. Using the same logic, perhaps dogs who are particularly noisy or active in their dreams are more stressed. Those who sleep soundly could be more relaxed. Sadly, we don't really know. Nonetheless, it's fun to imagine what your dog might be dreaming about.

Why does your dog sleep in such weird positions?

As well as being able to sleep anywhere, dogs often sleep in strange positions. To us, this looks uncomfortable and would leave a human with serious aches and pains. Your dog sleeps in unusual positions for lots of reasons. It reflects their personality and what they find comfortable, plus a good dollop of genetic heritage.

- **Back down, belly up:** Your dog might sleep like this when they want to cool down. The fur on their tummy is thinner so this position provides a bit of air conditioning.

- **Belly out:** Any position that exposes your dog's belly is a good sign as it shows they're relaxed. They feel safe enough to expose their vulnerable areas to the world!

- **Curled up in a ball:** This harks back to the sleeping position of your dog's ancestors. It's a position that conserves heat and protects their vital organs from being attacked.

- **Head on front paws:** In this position, your dog is most likely just having a quick snooze and is ready to leap into action at a moment's notice!

Just like you, your dog probably has a preferred position. It could be hanging over the arm of chair or legs akimbo. Even though there's an element of canine DNA at play, it does give you an insight into your dog's individual personality.

What's with the spinning?

Does your dog spin before they settle down for a snooze? (They will probably do the same before they poop.) Don't panic, it doesn't mean they're going off the rails! The way dogs go round in circles before they sleep is a throwback to their ancestors. When dogs lived in the wild, they would circle in tall grass to flatten a bed and scare off any snakes or insects that might be hiding within that area. The circling ensured they had found a safe spot to sleep. This behaviour is so deeply engrained that this is why your dog continues to do it.

Let them go round and round as much as they need. It makes them feel reassured. Rather than a personality quirk, think of it as a fascinating insight into how behaviour can be passed down through so many generations.

"A dog can show you more honest affection with a flick of his tail than a man can gather through a lifetime of handshakes."

Gene Hill

Around the house

Your dog loves being at home because, most importantly, it's where YOU are. But there's also so much else for them to do! What do your dog's house and garden-based quirks say about them?

Why is your dog obsessed with dirty laundry?

Thankfully, your dog doesn't have a strange fetish. Their penchant for dirty washing is due to their super-developed sense of smell. Like it or not, your laundry pile smells of you. In fact, to your dog's highly-tuned nose, it STINKS of you. And they love it.

Like many aspects of your dog's personality, this love of smelly t-shirts and socks is rooted in their past. Back in the days when dogs were wild animals, familiar scents helped them identify other members of their pack. By blending their own smell with that of their pack, dogs built strong bonds and a sense of belonging. Exactly the same thing is happening when your dog raids your laundry basket – they want to feel close to you and claim you as part of their pack. It's a compliment!

Disgusting bin antics

If your dog scavenges in your kitchen bin, it's both annoying and messy. They don't do it because they're hungry, greedy or lack a sense of self-respect. Dogs are natural scavengers and in their wild days they would have to find food wherever they could. Despite the fact you regularly feed your dog, their innate survival instinct is still there. Full of smelly delights (in your dog's mind anyway), a kitchen bin is absolutely irresistible, and if they find something edible and delicious in there, they'll become a regular visitor!

Putting the bin well out of your dog's way can help stop the scavenging. However, their amazing sense of smell means they'll probably find it quickly and try their luck again and again and again …

Why does your dog love to dig?

If you're a keen gardener (or would just like a backyard that doesn't look like a construction site), a digging dog can be a real pain. You'd be forgiven for thinking your dog does it to annoy you because as soon as you've filled one hole, they'll dig you another.

Some dog breeds are more natural diggers than others. Terriers and beagles are good examples of this because they were bred for that behaviour; to burrow and catch creatures like rats and rabbits. Yes, your dog is an individual to some extent, but all dogs carry certain ways of acting in their genes.

For example, when your dog buries a toy or bone, they're acting out how their ancestors would have buried food to save it for later.

Does your dog get bored easily? If the answer is yes, they may be digging for fun. Make sure you keep them stimulated and well-exercised and you may be able to stop them destroying your garden.

Household appliances

Does your dog have odd reactions to everyday household objects and appliances? Washing machines, brooms and, of course, vacuum cleaners can make dogs react in different ways. If your dog has a nervous personality, you may find them running for cover when you start your household chores. First off, a vacuum cleaner is loud. For your dog's sensitive hearing, the noise can be frightening. There's a strange thing moving around their space making an awful sound. Your dog's reaction could be to bark and growl at it, or even herd it, to assert their dominance. A less brave dog will simply run away and hide, overwhelmed by the stress.

If your dog has a more playful personality, their reaction could be quite different. They're more likely to be curious about vacuum cleaners and other moving appliances and attempt to play with them. Household chores will therefore take you twice as long to do!

A tale of tails

A big part of understanding your dog's personality is being able to interpret what they're trying to tell you. Obviously, dogs can't speak (if only they could!) so we have to rely on barks and body language to communicate with our pets. Your dog's tail is the most expressive part of their body and it has A LOT to say!

There is a common tail language among dogs. Curved tails can be a little harder to read, but generally tails are a great indicator of what your dog is feeling and thinking.

Tail wagging

Everyone knows that a wagging tail is a good sign. Some dogs wag their tail so hard that it shakes their whole body. When your dog wags their tail enthusiastically, in a broad sweeping motion, it is an expression of happiness and pleasurable excitement. Perhaps you've walked into the room or they've realised they're about to go for a walk. Deep joy!

However, a wagging tail can also be a sign of aggression. This is often the case if your dog's tail is tense and the wagging is high, fast and stiff. A submissive dog may also wag their tail quickly if they are cowering from a more dominant dog.

What's the angle?

The angle at which your dog holds their tail also provides clues to their emotions. When your dog is holding their tail high, they are feeling confident and happy. If the tail moves to a horizontal position, they are feeling less confident and more unsure (time to give them some reassurance!).

A tail that hits the floor or goes between the back legs either means your dog is trying to show subordination (indicating they're not a threat) or they are feeling anxious and afraid. Bear in mind the breed of your dog though. Some breeds, especially hounds like greyhounds, naturally keep their tail between their legs as that's their neutral position. It doesn't mean you should be worried about their mental state! For most dogs, a relaxed tail is held at around 45 degrees.

DID YOU KNOW?

Just like humans, dogs need to develop their communication skills. Tail wagging is a skill that puppies learn and master as they grow up. When a puppy reaches four to six weeks of age, they begin using their tail to talk, practising it with their mum and the rest of the litter.

Why does my dog chase their tail like a crazy thing?

The tornado that is a dog chasing their tail is incredibly funny to watch. If they're a puppy, tail chasing helps them to explore and learn about their body.

An adult dog will chase their tail for various reasons. It could be because they want to burn off some energy or are lacking mental and physical stimulation (a cue for you to up the levels of stimulation you provide). If tail chasing becomes a regular activity and you find it hard to stop your dog from doing it, it can be a sign of anxiety or irritation/discomfort in their tail area. Get them checked out by a vet if you're concerned.

Personality clashes

Do you get on with everyone you meet? No. Well, neither do dogs. Your dog will have their own likes and dislikes. And that includes the people, dogs and other animals they meet.

When you get a dog, especially a puppy, you can never be entirely sure how their personality will shape up. Fortunately, you can make a good guesstimate based on their breed (or breed mix). If you've chosen a breed known for its good nature and sociable temperament, it's likely your dog will happily settle in with the other pets in your household. Whilst some breeds are predisposed to getting on well with other pets, you should be able to introduce any dog without too many problems, regardless of the breed. What's important is introducing and socialising them properly, training, and being patient.

Anger and fear – the body language

If your dog has a dominant and assertive personality, it can lead to clashes with dogs of a similar disposition (and sometimes dogs who are showing zero interest in a rumble). Interestingly, a less brave, frightened dog will react in exactly the same way as an angry dog. Your dog may usually be meek and mild, but if they feel threatened, you could see a whole different side to them.

No dog really wants to have a fight. In most cases, their reaction is a preventative measure to make the threat go away, known as 'defensive aggression'. Your dog's first line of defence when they feel threatened may be to go into submissive mode. This is their way of telling another dog that they pose no threat.

What are some of the signs to look out for when your dog is trying to appear submissive?

🐾 Ears pulled back against head.

🐾 Sits or cowers with legs bent and hindquarters low.

🐾 Lies down or rolls over.

🐾 Spinning.

🐾 Yawning.

🐾 Drooling.

🐾 Trembling.

🐾 Rapid panting.

🐾 Tail between legs or held high.

🐾 Turns head away but keeps gaze fixed on the threat. This is called 'whale eye' – when your dog is looking so far out of the corner of their eyes that the whites of their eyes are showing.

If this fails to deter the other dog, or any perceived threat, your dog will switch to a more outwardly aggressive-looking mode and display these signs:

🐾 Ears rotated sharply forward.

🐾 Teeth bared.

🐾 Body held tight and rigid.

🐾 Stiff, locked legs.

🐾 Tail between legs or held high.

🐾 Growling that turns into snarling and snapping (lips drawn back from teeth).

It's important to be able to recognise these warning signs before things go too far. A dog will usually only attack if they feel cornered or that they have no other choice. Your dog will only be immediately aggressive to another dog if they've not been trained and socialised properly. If they haven't, then you have some work to do to fix that. Only then can you avoid situations that put your dog (and other people's dogs) in danger.

When too much is ... too much

If your dog is shy or anxious, meeting a more assertive dog isn't their only worry. They can become overwhelmed by friendly dogs that are too playful or boisterous. Your nervous dog might love playing with other dogs, but they know their own limits. When another dog oversteps that boundary (whether it be the type of play or its duration), your dog may feel the need to warn them off. Even if you know your dog's personality well enough to see this coming, when you see them react angrily for the first time it can be a bit of a shock.

Note that elderly dogs can be more irritable and will try to put younger, more energetic dogs in their place.

Flashpoints

Here are some examples of potential flashpoints with both other dogs and humans.

🐾 Competition over food.

🐾 Competition over toys or items they've found on a walk.

🐾 Competing for the attention of humans.

🐾 Blowing on your dog.

🐾 Children who don't understand how to behave around dogs.

🐾 If their sleep is disturbed suddenly.

🐾 Hugging them (really, dogs aren't keen on hugs!).

- Forcing a shy dog to socialise rather than taking it slowly.

- Any form of negative reinforcement that punishes your dog – this is NEVER going to make for a happy dog.

TEN DOGS THAT GET ALONG WELL WITH OTHER PETS

Here are some of the breeds that are known for their ability to live (peacefully!) with other pets.

Golden Retriever	Bichon Frise
Boxer	Cocker Spaniel
Poodle	Beagle
Labrador Retriever	Italian Greyhound
Cavalier King Charles Spaniel	Shetland Sheepdog (Sheltie)

"Everyone thinks
they have the best
dog. And none of
them are wrong."

W.R. Purche

Needy dogs and separation anxiety

Mutual trust is incredibly important for building a strong bond with your dog. But what if your dog is so attached to you that it finds it hard to be alone? Or they don't stop demanding your attention when you are there?

Why doesn't your dog like being alone?

Dogs like to have company. Without it, they feel vulnerable. Being alone affects some dogs more than others and will depend on their personality. If your dog is more nervous or they have previously been abandoned, they may be more prone to neediness and separation anxiety. Likewise, if they've got used to having you around constantly and that changes, it can be unsettling for them. Many dog owners will have encountered this after the COVID-19 lockdowns when life and work returned to 'normal' and pets no longer had their humans around 24/7.

Is your dog needy?

A needy dog needs constant reassurance. Even if you're there with them, they still demand your full attention – and won't hesitate to make this known! What should you look out for?

🐾 Following you around the house and not letting you out of their sight.

- Excessive barking or whining, especially if you aren't giving them attention or are leaving the house without them.

- Pawing or nudging you to notice them.

- Clinginess – for example seeking physical closeness by sitting on your lap or lying against you.

- Separation anxiety – see next page.

- Constantly bringing toys to you and wanting to play.

- Having difficulty relaxing or settling down without your presence.

Separation anxiety

If you have a needy dog, the chances are they'll also have separation anxiety, which can affect dogs whatever their personality. Even if they seem like a free spirit, there will usually be a point when your dog feels the need to come back to you. After all, you are the centre of their universe – and not just because you feed them and give them a warm, safe place to sleep!

Separation anxiety becomes an issue when you can't leave your dog alone without them feeling distressed. Signs of separation anxiety include:

🐾 Destructive behaviour (e.g. destroying cushions)

🐾 Excessive barking or howling

🐾 Accidentally weeing or pooping in the house.

Less common signs in your dog include trembling, excessive licking or biting (which causes self-injury), vomiting and not eating when they're alone. If your dog experiences separation anxiety, they might show signs of stress even before you leave them. When you get home, your dog is likely to be excessively excited to see you.

What can you do?

As much as you might love having your dog by your side, it isn't fair for them to depend on your presence for comfort. When you get a puppy, it's important to teach them to be alone as part of their training. If they learn that there's no need to worry about having solo time early on, it will normalise them being left by themselves and they're less likely to become stressed.

You can find lots of information online about how to gradually increase the time you leave your dog. Don't forget that your dog is an individual – what works and how long it takes will be specific to them. Follow their pace and never overstretch what your dog can manage too quickly. In fact, the more gradually you do it, the better – and more long-lasting – the results.

Tricks and tips to help your dog feel comfortable

Here are a few ideas to help your dog feel more relaxed when they're on their own in the house.

🐾 Take your dog for a long walk before you go out to burn off excessive energy and encourage them to relax or sleep afterwards.

🐾 Leave them with a special toy or chew so they've got somewhere appropriate to channel their attention.

- Close the curtains so they're not disturbed by anything outside.

- Put a radio on low volume to disguise any noises. (In fact, there are radio stations especially for dogs!)

- Turn off your electronic doorbell chime.

- If you need to leave your dog for more than four hours, get a dog sitter/walker or friend to stop in to keep your dog company or take them for a walk.

Fears and phobias

Like humans, dogs can be scared of the strangest things. Usually, it's something they haven't encountered before, such as an unusual noise. Their first response to a potential threat could be fear and uncertainty. Understanding how and why your dog is afraid of certain things can help you to help them overcome their anxieties.

Your dog can develop fears and phobias for a variety of reasons. These can be traced back to their roots as a wild animal, their individual experiences and also the characteristics of their breed. When your dog is frightened, they might shake, pace, whine, bark, cower, hide or exhibit behaviour that can be confused with aggression. (You'll find more on the signs to look out when your dog is feeling afraid on page 61).

Early socialisation

The critical socialisation period for dogs is between approximately four and 12 weeks. Socialising your dog means exposing them to people, places and situations outside the home. If they're not properly socialised in that time, they won't become used to the everyday world or understand what they don't need to be afraid of. Without early socialisation, your dog won't learn how to cope with new experiences in a positive way.

Bad experiences

If your dog has a traumatic experience, it can cause them to develop fears and phobias. For example, a dog that is attacked by another dog may become fearful of any dog, no matter how friendly. Or if a dog gets hit by a car, they might start to be terrified of all cars.

Learned behaviour (from you!)

Your dog can learn to be fearful of certain things if they see you reacting negatively. Do you panic if a wasp comes near you? Do you scoop up your dog if they go near an unfamiliar dog? Behaviour like that can easily transfer to your dog, so be aware of how you react to things!

COMMON DOGGY FEARS

Going to the vet

Vacuum cleaners

Loud noises (e.g. thunder, fireworks)

Going up and down stairs

Travelling in the car

Bees and flies

Men

Being left alone (see the chapter on Needy Dogs and Separation Anxiety on page 68).

Breed

Some dogs are more fearful and anxious due to their genetics. Border Collies, for example, are prone to anxiety. They're highly intelligent, get bored easily, need a lot of physical exercise and are very social, so if their needs aren't met in those areas, they become stressed.

How can you help your dog?

Don't force or coax your dog to interact with the object of their fear. Gradually expose them to the fear-inducing situation, but in a way that turns your dog's negative associations into positives ones. For example, if your dog is scared of car journeys, start with very short trips around the block and reward your dog with a treat and lots of attention. This way, they'll start to learn that a car journey can be a positive, fun experience. It takes time and patience, but you can flip their perception!

Active Archie or Lazy Luna?

All dogs need exercise no matter how long or short their legs! Some need more than others but it's crucial for your dog's overall wellbeing that you make physical activity part of their everyday routine.

People either love, tolerate or hate physical activity. It's fair to say that dogs are similar! You might find that your dog tends to be lazy (see page 79) or they might be at their happiest when they're sprinting across a field. As you get to know your dog's personality, you'll be able decide whether they're more couch potato or Usain Bolt.

However, if your dog is on the lazy side, don't let them dictate how much exercise you give them. Every dog needs to be active, in line with their age, health and breed.

Where do they get all that energy?

Don't confuse your dog's personality traits with the signs that they're not getting enough physical exercise. Do you recognise any of the following?

- Too much energy – your dog seems hyperactive or unable to settle down.
- Destruction – chewing, digging or destroying various household items.

- Weight gain (which can lead to health risks).
- Difficulty sleeping or restlessness during the night.
- Increased 'vocalisation', such as barking or whining.
- Pulling on the lead – trying to move faster or explore more.
- Difficulty focusing on tasks or commands.
- Behavioural issues – for example aggression and anxiety.

If you find yourself marvelling at how much energy your dog has (and are struggling to keep up!), consider whether they're getting enough exercise. Those overexcitable 'personality traits' may simply need burning off! Dogs struggle to manage and regulate their behaviour when they have unexpended energy. It's your responsibility to help them.

TEN HIGH-ENERGY DOGS

These breeds are perfect if you have an active lifestyle,
but be warned – you'll be doing a lot of long walks!

Border Collie	German Shepherd
Golden Retriever	Greyhound
Australian Shepherd	Dalmatian
Vizsla	Siberian Husky
German Shorthaired Pointer	Portuguese Water Dog

What can you do if your dog is lazy?

If your dog is lazy, you're going to have a battle on your hands
to get them moving, but it will be worth the effort. A lazy dog
will become a bored dog, an overweight dog and an unhealthy
dog. You need to be creative as well as patient. The key is to
show your dog how physical activity can be rewarding and fun.

- Start slow! Gradually increase the intensity of the activity,
  for example, by slowly extending the length of your walks,
  so that you don't overwhelm your dog.

- Find toys or games that your dog is interested in. If they
  don't like chasing a ball, they might love tugging on a rope.

🐾 Try different activities. Agility training is great fun and good exercise – both for you and your dog!

🐾 Go to different places. Playdates with other dogs are also a great idea – dogs love running and playing together.

🐾 Get involved! Your dog is more likely to be motivated to exercise if you're doing it with them.

🐾 Dogs love routine so if you make exercise a regular activity, they'll soon grow to expect and look forward to it.

🐾 Praise your dog for being active!

Understanding your dog's preferences will help you find the right approach to upping their exercise levels – and the healthier they will be. Even older dogs will benefit, but be mindful to not overdo things with them!

Boredom busting

Adult dogs have a level of cognition similar to that of an average two-year-old. And, just like a toddler, they get bored. Ensuring your dog's brain is stimulated is just as important for their health and wellbeing as physical activity.

Toddlers can tell you when they're bored. Deciphering when your dog is feeling the same is much trickier, especially if you assume their behaviour is just part of their personality. Getting bored easily could well be part of your dog's character, but if you don't help them combat it, their wellbeing could suffer.

Is your dog bored?

What do you do when you're bored? You might sigh, tap your feet or just flop in a listless heap. In many ways, a dog isn't so different. They will express their boredom through their behaviour. If you're asking, 'Why does my dog do that?', look out for these signs that your dog is lacking mental stimulation.

- Destructive behaviour – digging, chewing and destroying toys and household items.
- Barking and whining more than usual.
- Pacing or unable to settle.
- Lacking interest in toys and games they used to enjoy.

- Following you around and seeking constant interaction.

- Repetitive behaviour – for example, tail chasing and paw licking.

- Reacting quickly to sounds and movements.

- Changes in eating habits – consuming more or losing their appetite.

Get those cogs turning

Don't let boredom behaviours become an engrained part of your dog's personality. There's lots you can do to make them feel more fulfilled. You may even discover new facets to your dog's personality as you spice up their mental activity.

Exercise is an important part of boredom–busting. Taking your dog to a new place or on a different walking route can have brilliant benefits. They'll be able to explore new sights and smells that will get their brain and senses going. It's that simple! But if you want to explore more ways to get your dog's brain ticking, here are some ideas.

Target training: Teach your dog to touch a particular item with a part of their body. For example, ringing a bell with their paw when they want to go into the garden.

Vocabulary: Teach your dog to associate a name with an object. An obvious (and helpful!) example is teaching them to find and bring you your slippers.

Obstacle courses: Combining physical and mental dexterity, an obstacle course with jumps and turns will encourage your dog to think about how they use their body. Toys that are designed to challenge your dog's problem-solving skills are also fantastic for stimulating their brain and engaging their senses.

Puzzle toys: These encourage your dog to solve puzzles to access treats. They also teach them not to give up too easily.

Interactive toys: These make noises or move unpredictably, stimulating your dog's curiosity and keeping them engaged.

Snuffle mats: These conceal treats in their folds and compartments, prompting your dog to use their sense of smell to forage for goodies.

Chew toys: These aren't just for destroying. Some shapes are designed to encourage your dog to work out the best way to chew them.

Sensory toys: Any toy that has different textures, materials and sounds will stimulate your dog's senses, keep their brain engaged and encourage them to explore. (Also popular with babies!)

As much as dogs love routine, you need to keep their activities varied to keep their brain in tip-top condition. If they get bored, they are likely to get stressed and revert to demonstrating unwanted characteristics. Update and rotate their toys regularly to keep them interested!

Treat them well!

Remember, any kind of training and play is meant to be fun for you and your dog. Take a break if either of you get stressed or frustrated. Treat training as a game. Reward your dog with praise or a treat when they get something right. The better they get at responding, the less you'll need to use rewards. But don't stop using them altogether – your dog will be motivated by the thought that there just might be a treat involved, even if there isn't.

Use all these tools and tips and you'll have a brilliant time with your dog. It's a fantastic way to help you bond and it will bring out the best in both your personalities!

"Intelligent dogs rarely want to please people whom they do not respect."

W.R. Koehler

Zoomies

Charging full speed like a locomotive train, darting here, there and everywhere – welcome to the 'zoomies'. If your dog does it, you'll know it!

Zoomies are formally known as 'frenetic random activity periods'. While that description doesn't have the same ring to it, it does perfectly describe what zoomies are. Why does your dog engage in this seemingly crazy activity?

- It burns off excess energy, especially if your dog has been indoors for too long or they haven't had enough physical and mental stimulation.

- It's a sign your dog is EXTREMELY excited about something.

- Your dog is feeling pure joy!

- Zoomies can be a great stress reliever if your dog is feeling anxious or uncomfortable.

- It's an impromptu physical workout.

Zoomies can also be linked to your dog's natural instincts. Once upon a time, wild dogs would need to be able to run in fast, short spurts to avoid predators and to hunt. Zoomies are a perfectly healthy and safe way for your dog to express themselves. So, sit back and enjoy! Just make sure they're 'zooming' somewhere secure where they're not going to hurt themselves (or destroy priceless family heirlooms).

Is your dog a genius?

Every dog has its own wonderful personality. But do you wonder how clever your dog is? How do you know if you've got a doggy Einstein sitting in a basket in your kitchen?

What's your dog good at?

Dogs function at the same level as a two-year-old child. They're naturally social animals, so are fairly advanced in a range of areas. For example, your dog is good at understanding social signals (e.g. facial expressions) and gestures (e.g. pointing). They are also sensitive to emotions – just think of the wonderful way they give you more attention when you're feeling down. This demonstrates their capacity for empathy – the ability to understand and share the feelings of others.

What are dogs more average at?

Compared to other domestic animals, your dog isn't an A-grade student. Yes, they've got a fantastic sense of smell and excellent hearing, taste and touch, however they're no more intellectually advanced than other animals (and some are less smart than a pigeon). Your dog may be good at repeating tasks you teach them, but they're not so great at solving problems themselves. You'll also notice that they're not very accomplished at simple navigational tasks. Place an obstacle in front of your dog and watch them wonder how to get around it!

Why is your dog surprised when it sees itself in a mirror?

Does a dog know that it's a dog? It's a deep philosophical question, to which the short answer is 'no'. We know this because dogs are unable to recognise themselves in a mirror. According to research, ants can recognise themselves, demonstrating a self-awareness that dogs lack.

So, if your dog gives themselves a fright every time they encounter their reflection, don't worry – it's normal! It's an indication of limited intelligence, but it is endearing.

Does your dog have a memory like an elephant?

If your dog has a long memory, it's a sign that they're super smart. While you can't remember what you had for dinner last night, you'll be amazed what a clever dog can recall. Don't be surprised if you visit somewhere for the first time in months and your dog heads back to the exact same spot where they remember finding a ball. That trick you taught them years ago when they were a puppy? Chances are they still remember it. If they do, you've got a bright dog on your hands.

Why does your dog behave strangely when they see a suitcase?

When your dog is intelligent, they are also great at observing. They see a suitcase, put two and two together and reach the conclusion that you're going somewhere, also known as leaving them. Your dog is anticipating what's coming. (Then they'll try and climb into your suitcase.) If your dog knows when they're going to the V. E. T., it's thanks to the same process of observation and association. Clever pooch!

Why does your dog keep glancing at you?

When you're out for a walk and your dog is off the lead, you might notice that they keep looking back at you. That's a sure sign of a clever dog. If they're smart, they will look to you for guidance and instruction. This happens when they encounter something they're not sure about, such as another walker or an unfamiliar obstacle. They anticipate the situation and look to you for cues that advise them what to do.

TEN OF THE BRAINIEST BREEDS

Some dogs are cleverer than others thanks to their heritage and breeding. For example, dogs bred to follow commands, such as Collies, are more intelligent than those bred for power.

Border Collie

Shetland sheepdog

Poodle

Labrador Retriever

German Shepherd

Papillon

Golden Retriever

Bloodhound

Doberman Pinscher

Rottweiler

And bottom of the class?
Afghan Hounds are considered the least intelligent thanks to their low obedience level and unwillingness to respond to commands!

Is your dog risk averse?

Does your dog stop at the roadside before you ask them to? Do they stick close to you when meeting new people? If your dog steers clear of risks, they have a high level of intelligence. This isn't a bad thing if it helps keep your four-legged friend safe. Shying away from risk shows that your dog is cleverly assessing potential danger and acting accordingly. (See the chapter on Fears and Phobias, page 73 if this level of risk aversion is making your dog stressed.)

More signs that your dog is brainy

🐾 They have lots and lots (and lots) of energy.

🐾 They learn easily – you need to keep turning training up a notch to keep them interested.

🐾 They get bored easily (which might manifest as naughty behaviour).

🐾 They're so good at observing that they easily pick up bad habits. Especially from you.

🐾 They can follow your gaze and look to see where you're looking.

Happy hounds

We do everything we can to make our dogs happy, including things we shouldn't really do (such as feeding them titbits at the table). If our pet is happy, we're happy. It's a simple equation, and a wonderful one! So, how do you know if your dog is happy?

The closer your bond with your dog, the better you'll be at reading their emotions. For starters, if your dog looks like they're smiling, with their mouth open and tongue lolling over their lower teeth, they probably are. You can usually tell if your dog is happy by observing their body language and behaviour.

What does their body language tell you?

Let your body relax for a moment. You'll probably find that you sink into a neutral position. Dogs do the same. A happy dog has a relaxed posture and will hold their head in a neutral position, neither thrust forward nor turned to the side. Their tail will be loose and gently wagging. Ears will be in a natural position (not perked up or pinned back). Your dog's eyes will also looked relaxed – blinking is a sign of relaxation, and dogs often blink to calm themselves.

Playful and curious

If your dog wants to play, that's another sure sign that they're feeling happy. (Anything that gets you involved will bring them joy, of course.) They might bring you a toy or initiate play by bowing with their front legs spread out and bottom in the air, which is known as the 'play bow'. The fact that your dog is interested in playing and exploring its surroundings shows that they're engaged with life – and loving it. There's a lot humans can learn from dogs ...

Cuddles

A dog that feels strongly bonded to you will be a happy dog. If your dog comes to you to initiate cuddles and belly rubs, it's a sign they're feeling secure and content. When you interact with them in this way, your dog will absolutely glow inside. Notice, too, how they paw at you if you stop stroking them.

'Talking'

A happy dog will bark or whine when they greet you. In fact, your dog might create a whole range of high-pitched, excited noises that sound very much like they're trying to talk to you. It's pure, unadulterated excitement! It's a lovely thing to hear and guarantees you'll lavish them with attention and love.

Healthy and happy

Encouraging your dog's happy personality means giving them plenty of time and attention. However, any animal's happiness depends on their physical health too, so watch for signs they may be unwell. A healthy, happy dog will have bright, clear eyes and a shiny coat. A good appetite is also a positive indicator, as is sleeping well.

Remember, your dog has their own individual personality. This means that they may express their happiness differently.

CHECKLIST
Make your dog happy!

Most dogs are easily pleased. If they're fed, walked, kept warm and given attention, they'll be in seventh heaven. Here are some ideas to try with your dog that will help boost your bond. Tick them off as you go along. Your dog might not enjoy them all, so use your judgement – and make sure they're enjoying rather than tolerating your attention.

Pet your dog. It's good for both of you. Belly rubs are particularly popular if your dog is comfortable with it. Gently rub your dog's ears and you'll release their endorphins – the natural feel-good hormones that relax and calm your dog.

Raise your eyebrows and give them a relaxed smile – they'll recognise how happy you are to see them.

Groom your dog – it replicates the canine social behaviour that cements bonds in a family or pack.

Use 'baby talk' – dogs really love to hear high-pitched chatter from you. It will catch and hold their attention.

Have a sleep together. Curling up on the sofa with your dog shows them that you love them and will protect them.

Praise them for good behaviour! It's an important tool to motivate them so they continue to repeat their good behaviour.

Give them a job to do, for example waking up a family member. Dogs love feeling like a helpful member of the household.

Give them a massage. Done properly, this will benefit their health and happiness and build your bond.

Introduce them to plenty of new experiences – new places to walk, things to do and toys to play with.

Visit the groomers! Keep them tidy and clean and give them a pamper session. It's also very important to their health and wellbeing too.

Facial expressions

If you've ever marvelled at the range of faces your dog pulls in different situations, you won't be surprised to learn they have around 100 different facial expressions in their repertoire. Learning what your dog's expressions mean will help you understand and communicate better with them.

What does their body language tell you?

If your dog is calm and relaxed, their brow will be smooth (unless they're an endlessly wrinkly Shar-Pei!). When they raise their eyebrows they are, like humans, expressing surprise, but it can also indicate they're confused or feeling uncertain.

Head tilting

When your dog tilts their head to one side it can mean several things. They could be listening carefully to something – by tilting their head they can pinpoint the source of a sound more accurately. It can also be a response to a word they recognise – 'treat' and 'ball' being favourites! Or it can be in anticipation of something happening, for example, when you say, 'Do you want to …' and they hope you're going to finish the sentence with 'go for a walk?'

It's possible that your dog tilts their head when they are trying to understand what you're saying or doing. They're attempting to connect with you by interpreting your

emotional state and verbal or physical cues. Dogs are highly attuned to humans, and you can develop a truly amazing bond with your pet.

Bowed head

When your dog bows their head, it shows that they're waiting to discover what your reaction will be. You might see your dog do this when you catch them red-handed with the Sunday roast in their mouth! This expression is more common if your dog has an anxious or shy personality, or if they are submissive. (See also the chapter Guilty as charged? on page 122).

Mouth, jaws and teeth

Your dog's mouth area can also tell you a lot about what's going on in their brain. If there are lines around your dog's mouth, they could be feeling tense. On the flipside, if the area around their mouth is smooth, they're feeling relaxed. A chilled and happy dog will also have their mouth closed or slightly open. If they're feeling REALLY happy, your dog's tongue may be hanging out.

When your dog meets another dog, you might notice that they start 'smiling'. Some dogs will signal that they don't pose a threat by pulling their lips up to show their front teeth. This is usually accompanied by other submissive body language, such as rolling over. If your dog pulls their lips back, has a wrinkled muzzle (nose and mouth) and is showing their teeth, it is a sure sign of aggression. Remember that anger and fear can look very similar – see the Personality Clashes chapter on page 60.

Puppy dog eyes

Why does your dog's 'puppy dog' expression make your heart melt? By raising their eyebrows, your dog makes their eyes look bigger, like a child's. Faced with that look, our heartstrings are pulled, and we shower the dog with love and care. Dogs know exactly what they're doing, and we can't help but be sucked in!

For more on how your dog communicates with their eyes, go back and read the chapter, All in the Eyes on page 24. See also A Tale of Tails on page 57 to discover what an amazing asset your dog's tail is.

DID YOU KNOW?

Research discovered that dogs use more facial expressions when they are interacting with people. These include sticking out their tongues and raising their eyebrows. Rather than being unconscious movements, these 'special' facial expressions are reserved for us. It shows that dogs actively communicate and share their emotions with their humans.

"I once decided not to date a guy because he wasn't excited to meet my dog. I mean, this was like not wanting to meet my mother."

Bonnie Schacter

What's that noise?

Wouldn't it be fabulous if dogs could actually talk? Thankfully, your dog has a repertoire of barks for every occasion. The more you get to know them, the easier it is to interpret your dog's language and meet their needs.

Greetings

Your arrival home is one of the most exciting times of the day for your dog. Amid the blur of tail and fur, you'll hear a couple of mid to high-pitched short, happy barks. This is your dog saying 'hello'. If they are very excited to see you, you might be greeted by whimpering. It shows they're being submissive to you – their great owner has finally returned! If they are EXTREMELY pleased to see you, your dog's teeth may even chatter. This is a sign that they're completely overwhelmed by your arrival. There could also be a tiny puddle …

Don't expect your dog to greet strangers in the same way. Instead, they will issue several quick barks. This serves as an alarm call and is your dog's way of drawing your attention to something they don't recognise that you might want to deal with.

How to curb your dog's enthusiasm

It can be a problem if your dog gets too overexcited when greeting you or someone else they know. Excessive barking and jumping up is well-intentioned but you will need to work on curbing your dog's enthusiasm (people in general aren't especially fond of dogs who jump up at them and it can be upsetting for children). The best way to do this is to simply ignore them. Walk away from them, like another dog would do if greeted in the same way. Your dog will soon learn that exuberant greetings don't get rewarded.

TURN UP THE VOLUME!

Golden retrievers, well known for their intelligence and gentle personality, have some of the loudest barks in the dog world. The current Guinness World Record for the loudest bark is held by Charlie the golden retriever. His bark was measured at 113.1 decibels!

Growling

Growling is how your dog expresses annoyance and irritation. It sends a warning message that they're feeling nervous and uncomfortable. Listen up – stop doing whatever is making them feel that way or remove them from the situation causing it. Confusingly for humans, dogs also growl then they're playing or excited. This is common when they're playing with other dogs so don't suddenly panic that things are turning nasty. However, do be aware of other signs that indicate the fun is coming to an end, for example, your dog's body becomes tense or the growling escalates. This is the point to separate your dog from its playmate.

Does your dog growl when you try to take their favourite toy away from them, when something or someone encroaches on their territory or when when you're playing with your dog? This is 'possession aggression' and the growl is a warning. Back off and distract them with another activity.

Howling

Domestic dogs are able to howl, more commonly in breeds like Malamutes and Beagles, but most domestic dogs simply bark if they want attention. There are various instances in which your dog might howl. If they are experiencing separation anxiety, howling is one way to express their feelings of worry and isolation. Like whining, howling is also an expression of physical pain – if your dog doesn't usually howl and they're not themselves, it could be worth getting them checked over by a vet.

Does your dog howl when you sing? Don't be offended! High-pitched sounds can often set off a dog's howls. Don't be surprised if other dogs in the house – or even the neighbourhood – join in. This collaborative chorus is their way of feeling they belong to a pack.

Whining

Let's be honest, the sound of a dog whining can be quite irritating. If your pooch is a puppy, expect lots of whining. It's their main way of getting attention and communicating that they need something – just like a baby's cry.

For dogs that are past the puppy stage, stress and anxiety are two of the most common reasons they whine. It's how they tell you they're not feeling happy about a particular situation. For example, you'll commonly spot dogs whining when they've been left outside a shop by their owner. If your dog whines because they're worried, that's your cue to calm them down.

One of the easiest whines to identify is the 'excitement whine'. Accompanied by tail wagging, jumping and wiggling, it's a sure sign that your dog is totally losing control of its emotions! Your dog may also whine if they're bored. This is one whine to ignore, or you'll be making a rod for your own back. Provided your dog has plenty of physical and mental stimulation, there's no excuse for boredom whining and as difficult as it is to listen to it, try your best not to respond.

Why does your dog bark at thin air?

To witness your dog barking at 'nothing' is disconcerting. (And, yes, it's also a tad creepy – what can they see that you can't?!) Don't call the Ghostbusters straight away, because there are more mundane reasons why your dog does this.

🐾 Super senses: Your dog has very acute senses of smell and

hearing. It's possible they've smelt or heard something that us mere humans can't detect. Tiny movements, such as dust in the air or insects, can also be picked up by your dog and trigger barking. Again, these things are so small that we're unlikely to spot them.

- If your dog senses something approaching their territory, it will prompt them to bark. If they hear a dog bark in the distance, for example, their territorial nature kicks in.

- Some dogs simply bark because they're bored or feeling anxious. If your dog barks at thin air, consider whether they're getting enough physical and mental stimulation.

Remember, too, that your dog is extremely clever when it comes to getting your attention. If they learn that barking at nothing gets a reaction from you, they will repeat that behaviour.

Curious noses

Your dog's nose is incredible! They have around 250 million smell receptors in their nose compared to the mere five million that humans have. A dog's nose is their most important sense organ. It's no wonder then that their nose is such a big part of their behaviour.

Why does your dog insist on sniffing EVERYTHING?

Dogs like to stick their noses in everywhere. With one sniff, your dog can pick up all kinds of information from the smells around them. They can even tell the direction a smell is coming from by moving each nostril independently. For dogs, it's a perfectly polite way to greet and find out about each other. Your dog is naturally curious and you don't want discourage that.

Unfortunately, in the human world it goes beyond the limits of our social norms! The crotch area is full of sweat and scent glands so it's the best spot for a dog to gather information about a person. In the same way that your dog sniffs the bottoms of other dogs, they can find out personal details about the person, such as whether someone is healthy or what mood they're in.

If you want to spare guests' blushes, gently encourage your dog away or distract them. If you make too much of a fuss, your dog might associate sniffing human nether regions with getting attention, which will encourage the behaviour even more!

What's the weird thing your dog does with their mouth?

Does your dog flick their tongue out and lick the air at the same time as curling back their upper lip? They will often stop and do this when you're out for a walk. It looks incredibly odd but is in fact a natural response when your dog smells something particularly interesting. To give it its proper name, it's the Flehmen Reaction. Your dog picks up particles with their tongue and transfers them to the 'Jacobson's organ' on the roof of their mouth. This unique organ allows your dog to combine taste and smell. It gathers a whole host of information for your dog to process. You just need to get past the fact it makes them look and sound like Hannibal Lecter in Silence of the Lambs!

DID YOU KNOW?

A dog's sense of smell is so amazing that it can detect medical conditions. 'Seizure and alert response' dogs can warn someone that they're about to have an epileptic seizure. By detecting changes in the smell of a human's breath, dogs can also detect if a person with diabetes has dangerously low blood sugar levels.

Love, sweet love

Dogs aren't called Man's (and Woman's!) Best Friend for nothing. Treat your dog well and meet all their physical and emotional needs and you'll create a loving, trusting bond. We need our dogs as much as they need us. What are the signs that your dog is totally besotted with you?

Lean in!

Have you ever wondered why your dog leans into you? If your dog presses up against you, it's a sign that they feel safe and secure. You're their protector and you're an important part of their 'pack'.

All smiles

Dogs do smile. It's a toothy, dopey look, but it's definitely a smile. If your dog does this, smile back! They will receive your smile as warmly as you did theirs.

Eye contact

When your dog stares deeply into your eyes, feel free to melt – it's a good sign. Prolonged eye contact shows that they love you and trust you. You make them feel safe. As your dog looks at you, their brain releases oxytocin – the 'love hormone'. It's the same hormone that helps a mother bond with her newborn baby.

More surefire signs of love ...

🐾 'Borrowing' your shoes and clothes so they can feel close your scent.

🐾 Trying to sleep in your bed.

🐾 Checking in on you to make sure you're still nearby.

🐾 Showing concern for your safety.

🐾 Bringing you toys (they even trust you with them!).

🐾 Licking – basically, dog kisses – to nurture and groom you.

🐾 And last but not least ... showing immense excitement when you enter the room, even if you've only been gone for a few seconds!

Every dog has their own personality and will show their love for you in different ways. Don't be disheartened if they don't show ALL the signs above. If you pay attention to your dog's specific behaviours and when or where they occur, you will quickly understand how they express their love for you in their own special way.

"The world would
be a nicer place if
everyone had the
ability to love as
unconditionally
as a dog."

M. K. Clinton

Canine sixth sense

Have you ever thought that your dog has uncanny abilities? Do they have a sixth sense? Are they barking at thin air, or seeming to sense something before it happens? Dogs can often leave us perplexed. Is there something mysterious at work or are dogs just finely attuned to humans and the world around them?

How does your dog know when someone is coming home?

If your dog becomes unsettled and sits near the front door when a family member is due home, you might be wondering how on earth they 'know' this. They can't read the clock to tell they time. And they certainly can't message them for an ETA! So, what's going on?

Your dog doesn't have a psychic insight into the unknown, but what they do have is a sense of time. Dogs love predictability and they will quickly learn the routine of your household. They don't know for sure that a family member is due to arrive home. What they do know is that someone usually arrives back at roughly that time and they make a pretty good guess based on their internal clock.

It could also be that an association sparks the expectation of a homecoming. For example, you might always put the kettle on just before your partner gets home. Remember, too, that you might not hear someone walking down the path, but your dog's fabulous hearing means they most certainly will.

Can your dog tell if a storm is on the way?

Your dog's amazing senses are swooping into action again! They can detect the incredibly subtle changes in the air that indicate a storm is brewing which humans don't notice.

Changes in air pressure and an increase in positively charged ions can make your dog feel anxious, uncomfortable and restless. You might notice that they seem keen to find shelter. Your dog will also feel the static electricity a storm generates, especially if they have long fur. Again, this can be especially unsettling to them, and they can try to hide as a result. Their super-sensitive hearing means your dog will hear the distant rumble of thunder long before you do. Humans can 'smell' rain but your dog's sophisticated sense of smell means they detect the scent of rain well in advance of you feeling a drop.

For centuries, dogs and other animals have been known for their ability to detect earthquakes, volcanoes and natural disasters before they happen. As with storms, this isn't down to their ability to see into the future. It's those fabulous senses at work, hearing, smelling and feeling tiny changes in the environment that our less able human senses struggle to keep up with.

Dr Dog will see you now

When your dog senses that you're feeling unwell, you may notice changes in their behaviour. They might lick you more than usual, whine and be reluctant to leave your side. Your dog doesn't have magical powers, but they do spot the small signs that indicate their beloved owner is under the weather.

🐾 Illness can cause subtle changes in your smell, thanks to the presence of particular chemicals. Your dog can detect these changes before symptoms have even developed. They can also detect changes in your body temperature.

🐾 Your dog knows your routine inside out. As soon as that routine alters, for example, you spend longer in bed or are grumpier, your dog knows something is up and will become more attentive.

🐾 Dogs are very observant and are in tune with human facial expressions. If your dog detects that you're in discomfort, they know that something isn't right.

Last but not least, if you have a strong bond with your dog, they are attuned to your emotional state. It's the same as how we know if a family member or friend isn't quite 'right'. Your dog will quickly pick up any signs that you're feeling sad, unhappy or anxious and will behave accordingly. It's no wonder that they are used as therapy dogs. Their unconditional love and empathy means they can lift us up when we're feeling down and they never, ever judge us.

Guilty as charged?

If your dog has never looked at you with great big, droopy eyes when you catch them up to no good, are they even a dog? It's easy to transfer human emotions onto our pets, but are dogs really capable of feeling guilt? Let the jury decide ...

We know that dogs are capable of basic emotions. Happiness, fear, excitement and anxiety are all recognisable in our dogs. What we don't know for sure is whether dogs can experience more complex emotions.

The research

Believe it or not, researchers have actually studied whether dogs can feel guilt. A study by the University of Cambridge in the UK concluded that dogs aren't really expressing remorse when they look 'guilty'. What you're seeing is your dog's reaction to the negative emotions you emanate when you catch them being naughty. They are reacting to the tone of voice and gesture you use when you tell them off.

In fact, the university research found that the only time dogs look 'guilty' is when they're being told off. Rather than trying to say sorry, your dog is expressing a more basic emotion: fear. They probably have no idea what they've done wrong, they just know they've upset you.

What emotions can your dog express?

Did you know that dogs have all the same brain structures and emotion-producing hormones that humans do? An adult dog has the cognitive abilities of a two-and-a-half-year-old child – this means that their emotional development stops at that same age.

Your dog can therefore experience:

- love
- affection
- shyness
- suspicion
- happiness
- contentment
- anger
- fear and distress
- disgust
- excitement

However, your dog cannot experience more complex emotions, such as guilt, pride, shame and contempt.

Dealing with bad behaviour

No dog is inherently bad. There are only bad – or inexperienced – owners. In most instances, your dog is just doing what they think is right. Dealing with bad behaviour is not about trying to change your dog's character. Their personality is what you most love about them and it will shine through when they behave well.

Positive reinforcement

Positive reinforcement means deterring, or ignoring, bad behaviour and rewarding good behaviour. The idea is simple but not always easy in practice! Treats, praise and play will encourage your dog to repeat good behaviour – as well as repeating it more frequently. Negative reinforcement – for example, shouting or physical punishment – should always be avoided.

Exposure

By exposing your dog to situations where they are prone to poor behaviour in a controlled way, you can desensitise your dog to behavioural triggers. A prime example is getting them accustomed to being with other dogs. Take it slowly and get your dog used to situations gradually. Reward them when they do well and increase their exposure in small steps. This is particularly useful where your dog's bad habits are down to a lack of early socialisation.

Consistency

Change confuses dogs. If you're not consistent, you'll have a poorly trained dog with bad habits a-plenty. If you want your dog to respect boundaries, those boundaries must be firm and everyone in the house needs to reinforce them. Your dog will soon figure out if one family member is softer than another! Use a commanding, deep tone (but don't shout) when your dog is doing something unacceptable that you want them to stop. If everyone in the house uses this same tone, your dog is less likely to get confused.

Behavioural therapy

If you're really struggling to deal with behaviour problems and the steps above aren't working, it might be time to seek professional help. Dog behavioural therapists are trained in animal behaviour. They will assess your dog and identify the underlying causes of their issues. From that, they can develop a specific programme utilising a range of training techniques.

The effectiveness of any training always depends on the individual dog – some will respond better than others. You need to be committed and consistent, as well as patient and persistent! But all the effort will be worth it. With your dog, you're in it for the long haul – come rain or shine. It's a unique bond and you will always be there for each other. Treasure them!

CHECKLIST

When to worry

It is important to get to know your dog's personality and the characteristics that make them who they are. Not only does it help you meet all their needs and ensure their happiness, but it also lets you spot when they're not feeling themselves.

This checklist gives some pointers on behavioural changes to look out for. It is by no means exhaustive and is not a substitute for consulting a trained professional. If you have health concerns about your puppy or dog, contact your vet.

- Loss of appetite.

- Excessive scratching and licking.

- Lethargy and lack of interest in activities they have previously enjoyed.

- Changes in sleep patterns.

- Excessive barking or whining.

- Restlessness.

- Shaking and trembling.

- Pacing and circling.

- Anxiousness.

- Anti-social behaviour (especially if previously they were very social).

- Staring for long periods of time.

- Going to the toilet in inappropriate places.

- Not responding to your voice.

- Excessive tail chasing.

- Chewing and digging (where previously not an issue).

- Sucking at their own skin.

- Fear of, or an aversion to, something they previously liked.

"If I could be half the person my dog is, I'd be twice the human I am."

Charles Yu